Guard Your Heart with All Diligence, for Out of the Heart Flows the Issues of Life

HENRIETTA FREEMAN

authorHOUSE®

AuthorHouse™
1663 Liberty Drive
Bloomington, IN 47403
www.authorhouse.com
Phone: 1 (800) 839-8640

Published by AuthorHouse 09/19/2018

ISBN: 978-1-5462-5353-2 (sc)
ISBN: 978-1-5462-5352-5 (e)

Library of Congress Control Number: 2018909123

Print information available on the last page.

For my son, Jalen. I appreciate all you do but mainly for who you are. I am proud of the wonderful young man of God you're becoming.

For my daughter Cierra. I'm proud of the growth I see in you; so much more greatness in you is yet to be revealed through the Lord.

I love you both dearly. The Lord has great plans for your lives. Life isn't easy, but God is faithful, and with Him, all things are possible. I pray that you will keep Him foremost in your lives.

CONTENTS

ACKNOWLEDGMENTS

FIRST AND FOREMOST, I give thanks, honor, praise, and glory to God, because without Him, there would be no Henrietta or her story of overcoming life.

Lord, I am truly grateful for your everlasting love, grace, and mercy. Throughout my life and every trial, you never gave up on me. You made a way out of no way for me. You protected, healed, saved, and set me free in every way a person can be set free. You are my fortress, refuge, and strength. Apart from you, O Lord, I can do nothing, but with you, all things are possible.

This book is proof and I am a witness to what God can do.

I thank my family, friends and loved ones for their prayers and always being supportive of the work God has called me to do. To my mom and dad I give my love. To my dad Henry, I love you and Aunt Sharon. To my spiritual dad Pastor James Boyd, I love you dearly. Thanks so much for your encouragement, prayers, and wisdom. God bless you. To my sisters Mary, Bobbie, and Sharon my brother, Jimmy, my niece, Katrina, and a host of other loved ones, I love you all dearly.

To my uncle Willie Booker, author of Women at the Crossroads, thank you for inspiring and encouraging me and giving me a chance to witness you becoming a great author and seeing in me early on in life what I am becoming today. I love you and Aunt Betty.

To my pastors Apostle Michael and Prophetess Jenny Lock of We Are One in the Spirit Outreach Ministries, I am grateful for your support and teaching and for allowing the Holy Spirit to use you mightily to minister to me and the great congregation of We Are One in the Spirit. I love you both.

To Essie Sullivan, my sister in Christ and my dearest friend, thank you for all the encouragement and help you have given me; I am truly grateful for that. I thank God for blessing us to be on this journey together and to be able to witness the amazing work God is doing in each of our lives.

Keep moving forward in the work God has for you. I am proud of you. Love you. God bless.

INTRODUCTION

I WAS INSPIRED and encouraged by the scripture of Proverbs 4:23 so much that I decided to use it for the name of this book. For many years, my heart was left unguarded and unprotected from the turmoil that was caused by many issues in my life. Years later, I found myself dealing with the issues that had tainted me in my early years.

Oftentimes, when someone abandons, betrays, rejects, or hurts us in an awful way, instead of releasing those hurts, getting the help and healing we need, and deciding to forgive, we tend to hold onto those issues for years thus allowing it to build up plaque around our hearts. Harboring these issues can turn into bitterness, resentment and un-forgiveness.

Just like most people, I've had my share of trials and tribulations, but because I didn't guard my heart, I allowed so much hurt to enter it, and in turn, no good thing came out of it except most of my life's issues. Some were due to the poor choices I made, and others came into my life by no choice of my own.

For years, I harbored resentment and un-forgiveness in my heart not realizing that was damaging my spirit and soul. Harboring unforgiveness can bring on illness and keep you from living and discovering your best life, and even rob you of great opportunities and relationships.

As I dealt with the many issues in my life, I learned that what doesn't destroy you makes you stronger. That's exactly what happened. I grew stronger mentally, physically, and best of all spiritually.

Life will sometimes rob us of our peace and happiness through loss and other situations and circumstances that may be beyond our control, but we were meant to rise above our circumstances and not allow it to define us. We have the power to take it all back. We have to reclaim every bit of our joy and peace that the Lord intends for us to have.

I had to learn that life is what we make of it. We are not victims but overcomers through Christ Jesus! Today, I choose to live victoriously because the Word of God tells me I will have victory over life's trials and circumstances. His Word also tells me that I have been given authority to trample on serpents and scorpions (Luke 10:19), which means to me that I don't have to allow life's problems to gain a foothold in my dreams and goals. I can put my foot on whatever tells me I have to settle for less. I stand on the Word of God, and I trust the Lord will see me through every trial.

I am convinced that God desires us to be set free, made whole, and complete. He wants to give us peace—nothing missing, nothing broken. If you are discouraged today, I encourage you to take back whatever the enemy of life has robbed you of. The scripture of John 10:10 tells us that the thief comes to steal, kill, and destroy but that Jesus came that we may have life and have it more abundantly. Don't allow your issues to steal great opportunities from you, kill your dreams, or destroy your relationships. Instead, allow Jesus to give you life and give it to you in abundance.

Take back your future. Take back what life has robbed you of. If it's joy, take it back. If it's peace of mind, take it back. If you look around and your circumstances tell you that you can't, say, "Yes I can!" As you begin to discover who you are through a relationship with Jesus and through the Word of God, you will discover what you were created to do. Be ever encouraged; we were all born on purpose and for a purpose. In the eyes of the Lord, none of us are a mistake. Every life has purpose, so go get your life because your destiny awaits you!

CHAPTER 1

My First Father

I GREW UP in a single-parent home with my mother and siblings. My mother had six children. Today, there are only five of us. We lost our beloved sister Tammy many years ago. I now have one brother and three sisters.

I was the youngest of the bunch. Based on what I was told when I was young, I assumed that my father wasn't the same father as my siblings. Before my mother realized that she was pregnant with me, she had separated from her husband. After the separation, she began dating a man she was connected to for many years.

Not too long after she began dating him, she discovered she was pregnant with me. For many years, this man was whom I knew to be my father. I was his little girl, and he was my daddy. I was very young at the time my dad was in my life, so I couldn't recall many memories due to the fact that I was between ages one and four. My sisters shared with me their memories of him. They told me that he was loving, caring, and fun to be around; they loved him and he loved them. He raised my sisters as if they were his very own. I was told that when he and my mother were together, those were great times for the family but unfortunately, they were short lived.

After many years together, he and my mother decided to go their separate ways. It was hard on the girls. They didn't want to see him go. They really enjoyed having him around and spending time with him. At that time, I was still too young to understand everything going on; all I knew was that dad was no longer around. During these transitional times, things felt awkward and uneasy. My mother would let me visit him from time to time, but I felt funny about his new family situation. It wasn't that they didn't try to make me feel welcome; I just found it hard to understand everything that was going on.

At times I was withdrawn and kept to myself mostly. I knew I was not the only one experiencing feelings of confusion and worry, but for the most part, everyone tried to do their best moving forward.

I came into my own in my teenage years. At the time, I was living with my mother and one of my sisters. My other siblings had grew up and moved out of the home. I was very active at this point of my life. I took part in dance competitions and modeling. I couldn't carry a tune but I sure loved trying to. I loved Whitney Houston and Mariah Carey. I used to want to be like them so badly but of course singing was not in the cards for me.

I also enjoyed skating, which I became very good at. I was full of energy. I think my being so active kept my mind from going into certain places that were painful, therefore I became quite the entertainer. It was a way that I could escape issues that were affecting me. At the time, I didn't quite know how to deal with them.

As I got a little older, I began dating and going to proms, but I remember my dad not being around to check out the boys I dated, nor was he able to give me advice on whether or not I should date them. My mom would tell me that I better not come up pregnant!

During those times, I often felt I lacked my father's love and attention, but I never discussed with anyone how I felt about my father's absence in my life. I just kept my feelings and thoughts to myself. I would just tuck away the pain in my heart and keep on moving.

There was a point in time when my mother sought child support for me; in the process, a blood test revealed that my dad was not my biological father. I couldn't believe it. I felt like someone was playing a cruel joke on me, and I didn't like it one bit. At first, I didn't know what to think or how to feel about this devastating news. But again, I buried my emotions and feelings deep in my heart and never revealed to my family how I felt about this revelation.

My mother would often ask how I felt, but I really didn't know how to respond, nor how to express my feelings. She tried to explain some things to me as best she could but my mind wasn't comprehending them; I just didn't know what I felt regarding this situation. I still loved my father but it was all too confusing for me, therefore, I did what I knew to do best which was to bury my feelings in my heart and go on with my life.

Over time, I processed this new information as best I could, but it did not fix the brokenness that I felt on the inside. During one of my visits with my father, he told me that the blood test that proved he wasn't my biological father didn't change the way he felt about me and that I would always be his little girl. I believed that he still loved and cared very much for me. But I also felt that because he had a new family and that I was not his biological daughter, I would probably cause problems for him, so I didn't go to see him as much. It seemed very uncomfortable for everyone at the time.

Our communication drifted away over the years, and I saw less and less of him, but I eventually ended up reconnecting with him several years later. I was working for a financial company at the time when he came across my mind and I decided to get in touch with him. He told me it was all right to visit him, so I went to see him and brought my kids. He knew that I had had kids but he had never met them. When I finally got the chance to go see him, I could tell that he was glad to see me, and I was likewise. He and his wife were glad to meet my kids. We became reacquainted with one another. As he and I had an opportunity to address the past; he revealed to me how much it hurt him to know I wasn't his biological daughter. It hurt me just knowing that, but I thank God for the reconnection between us and our families. Even to this day, to me, he is still my father and I am still his little girl.

CHAPTER 2

My Biological Father

A YEAR BEFORE I graduated from high school, I wanted to know more about my biological father. My mother encouraged me to visit him so I could get to know him better. When I reached out to him, he was open to me coming to visit. Though he may have felt some kind of way about finding out that he had another daughter, he never displayed an unpleasant attitude toward me. He was a very reserved man. He kept to himself mostly, not wanting to be involved with a lot of people. He was single, and to this day, he has never remarried. Though he would never admit it, I believe he never gave up hope of getting back with my mother.

There I was, Mr. Freeman's daughter. I resembled him; I had gotten my nose from him as well as my slender, long legs, which I never cared for, but I knew where they had come from. I would never have admitted it then, but now, I know where my stubborn attitude came from as well. There was no denying he was my father.

The more I was around him, the more I saw that he didn't have many people skills. He didn't quite know how to express himself to me as my dad. He never once asked me how life was growing up; he just didn't seem to be interested, or maybe, like me, he simply kept his feelings and emotions to himself. He never revealed to me how he felt about having another daughter.

Over time, I saw similarities between our attitudes, and a lot of the times, our attitudes were what kept us from getting along well. We were too much alike in some ways, and that got on my nerves. Because of that, I felt I couldn't be around him very often, so I visited him only every now and then. Years went by, but our relationship remained casual. He often visited me and the kids to make sure we were doing all right. We would talk about the latest news or what was going on in the family, but we never talked about deeper issues that had affected me growing up. For some reason, I felt uncomfortable about bringing these issues up to him.

In 2010, he had a stroke that affected his entire right side. Thanks be to God, he recovered over the years, but he still couldn't quite take care of himself as he needed to, so I became his caretaker. At first, I wasn't thrilled with the idea of caring for him long term because I knew at times we didn't get along that well and would often butt heads.

While I was caring for him, I still did not feel close to him. We were living under the same roof, but he seemed miles away. Perhaps my heart was hardened toward him because of the things that he left unaddressed. I often asked my sisters how it had been growing up in a household with him, and they said that he had been strict and tough from time to time. I gathered that he hadn't been there for them emotionally or able to give them the love and validation they needed as well. He was a hard worker and a great provider, but he was emotionally unavailable. He never talked about his growing up much, but I feel he might have suffered from a lack of emotional and relational attention while he was growing up. It's often hard to give others what was never imparted into you.

At that time, I still had never heard him tell me he loved me or was proud of me for the things that I had accomplished in life. I had never received any affection from him though my heart longed for it. I did not want to ask him for his love and affection because it would not have been genuine. I waited for him to initiate those feelings for me naturally, but he never did. I did not realize it then, but all of the little rejections and what I didn't receive from my father had built up in my heart over the years. I felt that the things that were left unsaid is what hurt the most. Deep down, the little girl in me longed for that father figure who would spend time with me, teach me, sit me on his knee, and tell me how much he loved and cared for me.

CHAPTER 3

Men Issues

AS A YOUNG woman, I felt the need to be loved and validated, and I found myself looking for love in all the wrong places. I desired love, but I was conflicted about love. When I began dating, the guys just wanted to play games with my heart; they were not about giving me the love I desired. They told me they loved me, but all they really wanted was what they could get from me. They wanted someone to be there for them and meet all their needs, but when it came to my needs, they fell short.

There came a time when the games got old and I got tired of having my emotions played with so I turned the games around on them. I had had enough of the heartbreaks and the broken promises, so I decided I would treat men the way some of them treated women.

During this time, I began having unhealthy views of men. I felt that all men act the same way and that there was only one way to deal with them—to become like them. I thought that if I used them for what I wanted and did not care about their feelings, I could protect my heart. I displayed this attitude in my relationships. I wanted the control and to have the upper hand in everything and with every decision. At times, I became very cold toward them and would show them no mercy when it came to breaking up with them. I was quick to let them go when they messed up. I found myself displaying an "I don't really care about you" attitude and was often harsh with them.

I also limited my love and affection for them. If a guy messed up and messed around on me, I would find out about it and he would be gone so fast that his head would spin.

The guys I dated would often wonder how I could be so cold, but I felt that was the best way to protect my heart from being trampled on. Besides, I had many issues in my heart that I had not dealt with including low self-esteem, daddy issues, and the fact that I didn't love myself as I should have.

In a particular relationship that I had, I found it hard at times to receive the love that was being shown me, and it became even harder for me to give and express my love in return. I eventually compromised a serious relationship I had with a guy who truly cared about me and wanted to marry me. Due to the fact that I was dealing with internal issues, I was not able to fully commit myself to him. I had once heard that hurting people tend to hurt other people. I was internally wounded, therefore my relationship with the right guy didn't stand a chance. Along with every other problem in my life, I tucked away these issues in my heart and kept moving.

Today, I am grateful to the Lord for helping me achieve a more positive mindset and attitude toward men and relationships. I know that all men are not about mistreating women and not all women are about disrespecting men. There are many great and God-fearing men and women in the world who knows how to love and treat one another. I believe that when you love and respect yourself, you will attract positive people in your life.

CHAPTER 4

Self-Esteem Issues

WITH ALL THE other issues I had going on in my life, low self-esteem was simply another area in my life I was putting a bandage on and not dealing with. I didn't feel pretty enough, good enough, or loved enough, so I ended up looking for love, acceptance, and validation in all the wrong places. It was easy for fake love to show up in my life and mistreat me because I didn't love myself, nor did I realize what type of love that I deserved to have in my life.

When I was thirteen, I began taking notice of myself just as most teenagers do. I discovered some features I liked about myself and others I didn't like so much. When I was a child, I was teased about my skinny legs, and boy, that was the worst time ever. I never understood why I was so skinny, and it certainly didn't help that the neighborhood kids would call that out. For years, I wondered why God had made me the way I was and not some other way. It's funny how the very thing that you dislike about yourself is the very thing someone else wish that they had. I was more than willing to trade in my long, slender legs for shorter ones.

The older I became, the more I degraded myself. Most people thought I was attractive, but all I could see was what I wasn't and what I wanted to be. I became so focused on my flaws. When I began dating, I found out that some guys intentionally date girls with low self-esteem and insecurities often because they're looking for someone whom they can abuse in many ways. I know for a fact that I was a magnet for guys who had the wrong motives for dating me.

I dealt with self-loathing for many painful years. I hated having my picture taken. I would make sarcastic remarks about how I looked. I couldn't even accept compliments, and the list goes on. This was a very painful time in my life because I so wanted to love the person who had been with me all my life—myself. But something was keeping me from loving her the way she deserved to be loved and treated. I didn't realize I was carrying so much deep-rooted baggage that kept me from accepting and loving myself the way God had intended. While going through this period of my life, I didn't have a close relationship with the Lord, but I later found out that it would take His amazing love to heal, deliver and set me free from all the hurt and pain that I experienced in my past.

As I began to take a mental journey to my past, I thought about all of the hurtful things that I experienced in my childhood, teenage years, and even as a young, adult woman. I felt that these issues needed to be addressed in order to receive the healing that I needed in order to love and accept myself.

As I've mentioned before, one of the painful experiences of my past dealt with me not having my father around while growing up. We have often heard how important it is for young boys to have a father's influence in their lives while growing up, but I feel that it is just as equally important for young girls to grow up with a father's love and influence as well. A father's love is needed in a child's life, just as much as a mother's. In my opinion, a father should be the first male in his daughter's life to tell her that he loves her and displays to her how she should be loved and cared for. I believe that a father's influence in his daughter's life will have a great impact on shaping her self-esteem, building her confidence, and the way she view men.

I also believe that the kind of relationship a girl has with her father will also impact the decision she makes once she began dating and whom she will eventually marry. Whether most father's realize this or not, they play a huge role in portraying a positive male influence in their daughter's and son's lives and relationships

I remembered attending a women's luncheon where a dear friend of mine talked about self-esteem issues. I was moved in such a way that I felt like the Lord was using her to speak directly to me. I believe that every woman at the table received from her words what they needed for themselves; but I considered them to be life-watering words. My soul was so dry and thirsty in that area that I felt the Lord was releasing rivers of living waters into my soul. I was like Wow! This lady knows what she's talking about! She too had dealt with low self-esteem for years and had got the victory in that area of her life. She impressed me with her elegance when she spoke about who she was and whom God had made her to be; she knew who she was in Christ Jesus. She displayed much confidence; I thought she was very bold and courageous. I did not take her to be arrogant, she just simply knew who she was.

After that conversation, I felt like the Lord was telling me that it was time-actually, it was way past time—for me to deal with that area of my life. I realized God could not take me further in Him until I was healed and delivered from my past wounds.

I began reading the scripture of Psalm 139:13-16. As I meditated on this scripture daily, my old pattern of thinking was challenged by God's truth of what His Word says. His Word tells me that all of God's creation are fearfully and wonderfully made! That includes me and you. Through the transforming of my mind by the Word of God, I now know that God did not make a mistake when he created me. He uniquely designed us for His purpose. Marvelous are the works of the Lord! God does not make no junk, nor did He make a mistake on how he created us. I believe that whatever God made, it is worth looking at! For years I believed the lies of the enemy who told me that I wasn't good enough, wasn't smart enough, and that I didn't matter. Once I begun to understand the truth of God's word and who I was in the Him, the lies of the enemy no longer stood a chance of operating in my mind.

My family and friends began to take notice of the subtle changes with me. I began wearing skirts more often; before, I wouldn't dare show my legs, and those around me knew how serious I was about that. The more my mind changed about how I viewed myself, the more I began to love and appreciate what God had created when He created me. There was no more hiding or being shameful; I was actually loving myself in a healthy way. Over the next few months, I experienced pure freedom.

Many people today are obsessed with having the latest operation to enhance their body parts. It seems that everyone from Hollywood folks, reality TV, and people we know are having these cosmetic surgeries such as lip fillers, Botox, liposuction, breast implants, or butt injections. These surgeries can be very costly, and they can even lead to death if not handled properly.

We all have a right to change what we want about ourselves whether it's health related or just by choice, but I feel it is important to know that the way we were originally made was no mistake. We all like to look our best, so we lose weight, gain weight, we try different hairstyles, hair color and so on. However, I think that when we tend to go through such drastic changes because we dislike how we were naturally made or because of what others think, there may be underlying issues we are not dealing with.

Psalm 139:14 (KJV) says, *"I will praise thee: for I am fearfully and wonderfully made: marvelous are thy works: and that my soul knoweth right well."* Here, David, God's servant, was acknowledging that God knew everything about him. David knew that he could not hide from God, his Creator, and that there was nothing about him that surprised God. God knew his every thought and his every move. He had carefully knitted together every fiber of David's being that made him who he was.

Our Creator knows everything about us as well; not one inch of our frame is hidden from Him. We were formed in secret, and we were all fearfully and wonderfully made in the eyes of God. God doesn't make no junk, and I believe it is very important for each of us to love and accept ourselves and know our self-worth despite what anyone says or what the media tells us what we should look like.

Some people say they want to change their appearance because they're not happy with themselves while others say they want to do it to please their significant others. Let's look at these two reasons. I will use myself as an example. A few years ago, I wanted to change my appearance because I thought it would make me feel better about myself. I also thought that if I could simply change this or that about myself, maybe I would come to love myself. I was wrong; changing my appearance was not the real issue. The real issue was internal. No amount of makeup or surgery could even begin to address the deep levels of hurt that had built up like plaque around my heart over the years.

Some people say they want to change their physical appearance because that would please their significant others. If we feel that way, we need to understand why our significant others feel the way they do. People who cannot accept us for who we are may not be the right people for us or they might have their own issues they need to address. Either way, we should let them determine why they feel we're not enough for them as we are.

Many years ago, you would turn on the TV or read a magazine and see one standard of beauty. Today, however, there's a wide range of beauty being displayed in the media, not just one standard. If God took the time to make us, we are all worth looking at! I believe that beauty comes in every color, size, shape, and personality! African-American beauties come in a variety of shades. Caucasian beauties have different color eyes and hair. Hispanic beauties have their lovely accents and hair textures. Some women have full hips, lips, and backsides. Women's hair textures range from coarse and curly to wavy, thick, and thin. Some women are plus sizes and others are petite; some are tall, medium, or short. There is much variety and beauty to be seen in women. The world would be totally boring if we all looked the same.

All our differences make us who we are and unique; they are to be celebrated rather than ridiculed or shamed. Please don't ever allow someone to put you down and make you feel bad about your true, authentic self. The real you should be celebrated, loved, and accepted by you first, and yes, others also, but if someone does not love and appreciate you for who you are, that's on him or her. Don't let others' opinions keep you from being you. Loving and accepting yourself matters more than anyone's opinion. Be the best you that you can be because everyone else is taken!

I want to look at self-esteem in a different way here. It is a good thing to be able to love the skin you're in, and it's good to speak about outer beauty, but I believe real beauty comes from deep within. In the scripture of 1 Peter 3:3-4, we read that it's not the outward adorning of a person that's most important; his or her inner part is the most precious. People tend to look and judge others based on outer appearances, but God looks at our hearts. At some point, we all have probably had distorted views that caused us to make poor decisions in our relationships, but as we work on our issues and become better people, we will feel much better about ourselves inwardly and outwardly and attract people who mean us well rather than make us feel less than we are.

I've observed the men-and-women relationships of those close to me as well as my own. I've seen men choose petite women over bigger-boned women, curvy women over apple-shaped women, light-skinned women over dark-skinned women, drama queens over those with quiet spirits, and vice versa on all these. Do we choose partners based simply on outer appearances or what they possess? Men are visual by nature, but so many men have made poor decisions about women they date because they focus on their outer appearance rather than taking the time to get to know them personally. Because of this, many men have found themselves paired up with women with whom they have nothing in common, involved in baby mama drama, being locked up for not paying child support even when they were actually supporting their children, or just going through unnecessary drama for no reason.

And many women, including myself in the past, have chosen men based on how fine or sexy they were, how much money they have, or what kind of cars they drove. Some women choose guys with bad-boy attitudes and overlook great-hearted guys who are nice, respectful, and God-fearing. My male friends once told me that women don't want to date nice guys; instead women mostly date guys who cheat on them, disrespect them, give them babies but won't commit to marrying them, and so on.

Some of the attributes that attract us can sometimes lead us into trouble. We can be so attracted to these things that we see outwardly, that we can miss every sign inwardly that warns us that some people may not mean us any good. We have an enemy called Satan. He knows what we love and what turns us on, so all he has to do is dress it up in a pretty package and send it our way to wreak havoc on our lives.

We as women, have to be careful about smooth talk, nice abs and biceps, fine facial features, a shiny car, a big bank account, and that bad-boy attitude. Some of us may be attracted to that, but if there is something wrong with a man's heart, none of those attributes will do us any good. Too many women have found themselves involved with womanizers, abusers, drug dealers, child molesters, drunkards, and so on. These things might not be evident at first, but the longer you date someone, the more their true nature will show.

And men must be careful. If men would take the time to get to know women—who they really are on the inside—they would have a better chance of finding women who care more about them than what they are driving or the size of their bank accounts.

Most men love curves, but some women with curves can be as mean as the devil and cause them all kinds of heartache and drama. I am not saying that all fine men with big bank accounts or beautiful women are evil; I mean that some of them could have flaws lurking behind their attractiveness. It is not good to make long-term commitments based on what we see outwardly; it is well worth taking the time to get to know a person inwardly.

For those who may be struggling with low self-esteem, I pray that you take the time to read and get to know what the word of God says about you and that you come to experience the type of freedom that I have.

I want to share some scriptures with you that you can meditate upon daily.

John 8:36
1 Peter 2:4-6
2 Corinthians 5:17
Romans 12:2
Colossians 1:13-14
Ephesians 1:7
John 15:5
John 1:12

These powerful scriptures gives us all the validation that we need. If you have ever confessed your sins and believed in your heart that Jesus died for you, and you have accepted Him as your Lord and Savior, then you are now a new creation in Christ Jesus. You are loved and you have the approval, forgiveness, and even an inheritance from the Lord, Jesus Christ. Once your mind becomes renewed by the Word of God, the Lord will set you free from the negative thoughts and criticism of yourself and from others. Whom the Son sets free is free indeed! Jesus loves you and He made no mistake in creating you. You are fearfully and wonderfully made!

CHAPTER 5

Holes in My Heart

I ONCE HEARD my former Pastor say that growing up without either parent can leave an individual with incompleteness within their life structure. He talked about the importance of receiving specific things from both parents that otherwise without it, it could create issues later on. For example because I missed a period of many years without having a father/daughter relationship, I feel that it left certain voids in my life that I later tried to fill with things and people that were not good for me.

Growing up with one parent in the home can create issues of incompleteness within the life structure later on in life. Not having a father figure in the home while growing up, left holes in my heart. My former Pastor had described it as trying to fill up a bucket with water, to only get to where you're going and find out that the bucket is empty. Years later would prove that I couldn't hold the love that was being poured into me at certain times in my life. I was conflicted about love. There was so much that I didn't quite understand about love. I didn't know how to receive it, nor did I know how to give it. I didn't feel worthy of love. I had trouble loving others as well as myself. And because I didn't seek help to mend the broken places of my heart, I jeopardized and ruined great relationships because my heart couldn't hold the loved that was being poured into it.

We can go through life with our hearts leaking and not realize it. We have to address the hurtful things that left us with internal scars at some point or else, when something good comes along, we will end up jeopardizing or rejecting it. We can't afford to go through life leaking because there is too much love to give to and receive from others, and we have a lot of living to do. Unresolved bitterness and unforgiveness can hurt our potential to be loved and love others.

When others try to love us in every way they can, it can be hard to retain the love and all its positives if we have leaky places in our hearts. Sometimes, we may think that it's impossible for others to really love and care about us or that we don't deserve to be loved; that attitude can stem from the brokenness we feel based on our pasts.

It's important that we learn to forgive along the way and get the healing we need. If we continue to put bandages over those leaky places in our hearts, we will never experience the kind of love, joy, freedom, and prosperity we were meant to have. Life will continue to rob us of what is rightfully ours if we don't get the deliverance and healing we need.

I am learning now more than ever to guard my heart from the unforgiveness and bitterness that tends to creep up on me when I least expect it. We can't often shield our hearts from the subtle attacks that come our way through hurtful people or circumstances, but we can decide to quickly forgive so that bitterness will not take root in our hearts.

It is best to retain all the good life has to offer us and release the bad. We live and learn; we grow and mature, but the wisdom that comes from the ashes of life were meant to be shared with others to give them hope that they too have much to live for and that they do not have to go through life leaking.

CHAPTER 6

Domestic Violence

DOMESTIC VIOLENCE IS described as the willful intimidation, physical assault, battery, sexual, and other abusive behavior as part of a systematic pattern of power and control perpetrated by one intimate partner against another. It often includes but is not limited to physical violence, sexual violence, psychological violence, and emotional abuse.

Domestic violence can and does affect individuals in every community regardless of age, economic status, sexual orientation, gender, race, religion, or nationality. If left unaddressed, it can result in physical injury, psychological trauma, and in severe cases even death. Domestic violence stems from a desire one person has to maintain power and control over another.

Statistics[1*]

- One of three women and one of four men experience intimate-partner physical violence, sexual violence, or stalking in their lifetimes.
- Domestic violence is the leading cause of injury to women—more than car accidents, muggings, and rapes combined.

---

[1] * https://ncadv.org/statistics.

- One in five female high school students report being abused by a boyfriend (American Medical Association).
- On average, nearly twenty people per minute are physical abused by an intimate partner in the United States.
- Most domestic violence incidents are never reported.

> He will rescue the poor when they cry to Him; He will help the oppressed, who have no one to defend them. He feels pity for the weak and the needy, and He will recue them. He will redeem them from oppression and violence, for their lives are precious to Him.... (Psalm 72:12-14)

In His mercy, God does not allow violence and oppression to continue unchecked. Domestic violence hurts the heart of God and it is in stark opposition to God's plan for families. He is not unmoved by its victims, nor has He abandoned them. His plan for human relationships—particularly those among family—is a beautiful depiction of who He is. Family is meant to reflect God's love. It saddens Him when a home turns into a place of pain. God's desire for those involved with domestic violence-both victims and abusers-is healing and wholeness (Crosswalk. com and Got Questions.org).

When I was growing up, I often heard stories about some of my family members being involved in abusive relationships. I even witnessed my mother going through some form of abuse with her boyfriend. At the time, I was young, and I thought what a horrible thing for anyone to have to go through. It never crossed my mind that I would one day find myself involved in an abusive relationship too.

At one point in my life, I had such a desire to be loved but didn't love myself enough to know what kind of love I deserved. I ended up in two abusive relationships. The first abusive relationship that I was involved in mainly involved verbal abuse. Of course it didn't start out that way; it never does. Everyone puts his or her best foot forward at the beginning of a relationship, but somewhere down the line, things can take a turn for the worse.

Verbal, mental, and emotional abuse can be just as bad as physical abuse. Emotional abuse leaves internal scars that you have to deal with long after the relationship is over. It is also damaging to one's confidence and self-esteem; it chips away at your self-worth bit by bit. Emotional abuse can leave an individual wounded for years. I've spoken with people who didn't even know that they were being verbally abused because they associated abuse with having physical scars. Emotional and/or mental abuse may not carry physical scars but it doesn't mean that you don't have internal scars. It's important for people to surround themselves with positive people after they have left an abusive relationship for many reasons, but it's critical that an individual's self-worth and self-esteem be built up after the constant criticism, lies and put-downs that he or she has endured.

After I ended the relationship where I was being verbally abused, later on I began dating a guy who I later discovered had the same abusive tendencies. The signs were not visible at the beginning but after a year of dating is when the verbal abuse started, as well as pushing, hitting, threatening and even kidnapping. I realized I didn't take the proper time to recover and heal from those internal wounds I had suffered in the previous relationship, nor did I realize I deserved so much better. This individual had issues from his childhood that he never addressed, and they began to surface during our relationship. That time, it was more verbal abuse and even physical abuse along with kidnapping. I endured six years of verbal and physical abuse as well as repeatedly being threatened if I ever left the relationship.

As I began to have children, I realized that this situation was no longer just affecting me, but now my children were involved, and they were witnessing the abuse that my brokenness had led me into. It did concern me of what I was subjecting my children to. I didn't want my son growing up thinking it was okay for him to put his hands on a woman, and I didn't want my daughter growing up thinking it was okay to be with a man who abused women. I knew I had to leave, but at the time, I didn't know how.

This individual and I would break up several times and eventually I would go back to him and listen to his lies about how he was sorry and would never do it again, but it would always happen again. I was locked in that cycle for years. I was miserable while I was with him, but when we were apart, all I knew was that I wanted to be with him as crazy as that sounds. My friends and family would ask me why I kept going back to him; I honestly didn't know. I felt that I was caught up in a cycle that I could not break on my own.

Today, I truly believe in the power of prayer. Back then while I was involved in that toxic relationship, I didn't know how powerful prayer was but I knew that I had a mother who truly believed in prayer and I knew that she prayed for me all the time. Once this cycle of going back and forth with my ex was broken, I began to feel hope for my kids and I and that we could live a life free of bondage. As my thoughts began to change, so did my actions. After the final break-up, I left him and I never went back. I didn't feel a pull on my soul to go back to him this time, and I stopped fearing being apart from him. I believe that through my mother's prayers, God changed the way I viewed him and the whole situation. I eventually left the relationship and never looked back. I thank God for hearing the prayers of my family and friends. He turned the situation around and kept me and my children safe during that transition.

Overtime, I have observed the reasons why some people tend to stay in abusive relationships, including my own personal reasons why I feel that I stayed and endured the abuse. Here are some reasons:

Fear. Some people tend to stay because they fear what will happen to them or their loved ones if they try to leave.

Lack of money. Some people rely on their abuser's income. They fear that they can't support themselves and that they may become homeless.

Believing things will change. A person hopes that their partner will get help and change.

Embarrassment and shame. Some people don't want their family and friends to know what they are going through. They often paint a picture that all is well in their relationships even though it's not.

Low self-esteem. People can tend to think that it's their fault that they are being abused or they may feel like they can't do any better than the person they are with. They may even feel that they are not even worth being loved.

Family. Some people stay in toxic relationships just to give their children the chance to grow up in a home with both parents. Actually, this can be more damaging to the children.

Religion. Some people feel that it is against their religion to separate from their spouse.

No matter the reason why people choose to stay in abusive relationships, nothing is as important as their life and the lives of their loved ones. Some people feel there is no way out, but I am a living example that you can get out, all praise be to God. There are many organizations that are available to help provide a safe place to stay after individuals have escaped their abusive partners. Too many people have lost their lives by remaining in these relationships either through a lack of knowledge, fear, or a lack of belief that they could receive help to escape their abusers. No one deserves to go through or deal with such devastation and bondage. We are all worth so much more. Jesus did not give up His life on the cross for us to be someone's doormat, punching bag, or a way of escaping his or her issues. There is hope and there is help in finding freedom we all deserve.

Upon speaking with individuals about domestic abuse from time to time, I noticed how some people are not aware that they were even involved in an abusive relationship. As mentioned earlier, physical abuse is not the only form of abuse. I want to share with you four types of abuse and some examples of each of these so that you may be more aware of them.

Physical abuse: Physical force is often used with this type of abuse. If you are being punched, slapped, kicked, bitten, or choked, then you are experiencing a form of physical abuse.

Emotional/Mental abuse: With emotional/mental abuse comes verbal offenses. If you are being bullied, threatened, manipulated, controlled, criticized, intimidated, or shamed, you are experiencing a form of emotional and mental abuse. Emotional abuse is not always recognized at first because it can come about in a subtle type way.

Financial abuse: Most people don't always recognize that they are being financially abused but here are some examples. Your partner may try to keep you from making enough money to support yourself or keep you from becoming independent. That individual would rather have you depend on them for your needs often so that they can control you. An individual can also try to keep their partner from being promoted on a job and even go as far as being watchful of how much money you make and how much you are spending. Sometimes the individual won't even allow their partner to have a bank account.

<u>Sexual abuse:</u> Sexual abuse involves a person being taken advantage of in a sexual manner. If you do not give another individual your consent for sexual activity, then you are considered being sexually abused. An individual can also inflict pain on the victim during sex as well as pass on sexually transmitted diseases often times by refusing to use protection.

All types of abuse are wrong. It doesn't matter what kind it is or who it comes from, just know that it does not have to be tolerated.

If you or someone you know is currently in an abusive relationship, please get help. Reach out to someone you can trust. Many organizations are available to assist individuals who are needing a place to go after leaving an abusive environment. You do not have to live your life in fear and oppression. Your life is worth so much more. You too, can start life anew and live in the freedom and peace that you desire.

CHAPTER 7

Light at the End of the Tunnel

YEARS AGO, I had felt my getting to know the Lord was on a casual level. I didn't attend church on a regular basis, therefore, cultivating a close relationship with the Lord wasn't exactly at the top of my priorities. I didn't have a close relationship with the Lord, but I knew He was real. During those times when I was involved in the abusive relationships, I knew that my mother was praying for me and I knew the Lord had heard her prayers because of how He brought my kids and I safely out of the abusive relationship that I was involved in.

When I was young, I attended church regularly with my mother and siblings. I was saved and baptized at age seven. Back when I attended church with my mother, the women who attended this church could not wear jeans, only dresses. My mother's job as a painter called for her to wear jeans and that did not sit well with the leaders of the ministry. At the time, she was a single parent and the family's sole bread winner; she knew that she had to keep her job, so she felt she had no choice but to leave our church home. Over the years, she visited other churches but she never became a member. I believe the incident really hurt her and made her feel uneasy about joining another church, so she never did.

Fourteen years went by before I began attending church regularly again. I eventually decided to join a church with a friend of mine and thus began a journey of getting to know the Lord. I heard my family talk about the Lord from time to time over the years, and I would often hear passionate testimonies coming from people I attended church with, but I didn't know the Lord as well as they did. I often wondered when I would grow to a place where I would be passionate about the Lord the way I saw that others were.

I attended church each Sunday and Wednesday bible study for years. I kept to myself a lot during those years; I kept people at bay, never letting anyone get close to me—even those at church. At the time, I didn't know why I had such a strong desire to keep myself isolated. I guess I had been wounded by people so much through the years that I just didn't desire to be close with most people. I would show up at church, put my church face on, smile, and pretend everything was okay. But everything was not ok. I was dealing with some heavy heart issues that I didn't want anyone to know about. I would go through the routine of service and head straight home. No one knew it, but I was sinking more and more into a state of depression.

I was good at pretending to be all right, but my heart was wounded, and I couldn't deny that. I didn't realize that the abuse I endured from past relationships; issues that I had with my father; and many other issues were all taking a toll on my heart.

I felt I had to be the strong one for some of my family and friends. I felt I couldn't afford to be transparent and vulnerable because I had to be there to support others who needed to talk to someone about their problems. While I was helping keep other people strong, I would ask myself, *"Who's going to hold me up"? "Who will have my back"? Who will allow me to fall apart in their arms and be vulnerable when I need to be"?*

On top of everything else, I had to be strong for my kids because I was now the mother and daddy to my kids as well as the head of the household-which meant to me that I was responsible for taking care of everything! At one point, raising my kids as a single parent was starting to take a toll on me. All these things were building up to a pressure that my heart was never meant to bear. Instead of releasing all of the hurt and letting go of past issues, I just kept going on with life, pretending everything was alright while I was slowly falling apart.

My stubbornness and pride often got in the way when people offered to help me; I felt like I was even rejecting the Lord's help at times. I yearned to get close to the Lord but I kept focusing on everything that was going wrong in my life. I tried reading my bible, going to church, and praying, but I couldn't seem to let my guard down and allow the Lord to come into my heart to heal me. I can now see how the weight of my problems and issues had me bound and depressed so much so that I had contemplated taking my life.

During these hard times, I never told my family or friends what I was going through because I felt they would never understand. Life seemed great for everyone else but I felt like I was a magnet for adversity. All I knew was that I wanted it all to be over. Though I was to the point that I wanted to take my life, there was always something that wouldn't allow me to do that. There was a light at the end of the tunnel...

I went back to college in 2009. I had attended college after graduating from high school but had dropped out because I wasn't sure what I wanted to major in. While I was attending college the second time around, I was going through a depression period. One day, I left class and was driving home on the highway; a thought crossed my mind— just let go of the steering wheel and let whatever happens happen. My eyes began to fill with tears, but I didn't give in to that mean voice in my head that was trying to make me take my life.

I made my way home and saw my neighbor unpacking her groceries. I hurried over to ask her if she would come pray for me. I knew this woman was a woman of God; she was always very kind and always helping others. She would often have gatherings at her place where women could come together for prayer. She had invited me to come numerous times, but I never had. But then, I knew I needed her because I was in trouble. I trusted her to pray with me.

As we came together before the Lord in prayer, I began to feel the pressures of life lift off my shoulders. I broke down and sobbed like a baby. But afterward, it was like a peace began to come over me that I could not explain or understand. All I knew was that I felt things were not as bad as they had seemed before. For the first time in a long time, I felt things were going to be all right. That was the power of the Lord.

I knew God had heard our prayer. I believe He had been waiting for me to release all my pressing burdens to Him. Once I released them, even through tears, I felt more weight lifting. I didn't realize it then, but the Lord had had my back the entire time. In His presence, I felt safe enough to release all the hurts, betrayals, rejections, and issues that I ever had. With the Lord, I could be vulnerable and transparent. I could hide nothing from Him because He already knew everything about me and every heartbreak that I had ever experienced.

At the time, I had been weary of all of life's problems that I was carrying over the years. Once I discovered that Jesus had been there for me all the time and that He was simply waiting for me to grasp that truth, I saw light at the end of the tunnel. This amazing truth is spoken of in Matthew 11:28–30, which is meant for all who are weary of carrying around their burdens and feeling hopeless. There is hope in the Lord. Only in Jesus have I found a place to rest my burdens. Jesus is waiting to help all of us with every issue we have; nothing is impossible for Him.

Shortly after my deliverance took place, things began to turn around in my personal life as well as my spiritual life. I decided to rededicate my life to God. I was baptized again. When I was baptized at age seven, I didn't quite understand the full meaning of it all. I am now fully aware of what my Savior did for us all on Calvary. After I rededicated my life to Christ Jesus, I began to see things differently. I began to thirst after the spiritual life, and I had a desire to read the Bible more than ever. I started going to some of my neighbor's monthly prayer meetings, and I even began to open up to people and develop new friendships. As the Lord continued to set me free, I opened up all the more to the possibilities before me. That was a time of transformation and a new beginning for me.

Falling in love with Jesus was the best thing that ever happened to me. I was experiencing real love, the kind my heart had always longed for. I call it agape love. According to Wikipedia, agape is a Greco-Christian term referring to love. It is the highest form of love and charity; it is the love of God for humanity and humanity for God. It is an unconditional love that transcends and persists regardless of circumstances. You will find love most beautifully expressed in 1 Corinthians 13:4–8.

I had been looking for a love like that for many years, but as I mentioned, I was looking in all the wrong places. I was looking for it in my parents, relationships, friendships, and family. Not that any of them was incapable of loving me; it was just that my heart was in search of a much deeper love, the kind of love that would allow me to be my authentic self and not have to pretend or try to be perfect for fear someone would stop loving me if I wasn't. I was in search of the kind of love that would be here today and not gone tomorrow for whatever reason. I wanted the kind of love that no matter how imperfect I was, it would not judge or abandon me. My relationship with my Lord and Savior Jesus Christ allowed me to experience this amazing love. The more I trusted in the Lord and became closer to Him, the more I experienced His perfect love.

If you have found yourself weary of searching for love in all the wrong places, or if it seems that nothing or no one can satisfy your inner thirst for love, acceptance, or forgiveness, let me encourage you to open your heart to Jesus today. If you've never accepted Jesus Christ as your Lord and Savior, then I would like to share with you how. Pray this prayer with all of your heart. "Dear Heavenly Father, I confess that I am a sinner and that I have sinned against you. I ask you to forgive me for all my sins and I choose to follow, obey, and accept your son Jesus Christ as my Lord and Savior. I believe in my heart that your son Jesus Christ died on the cross and payed the price for my sins. I believe that He rose on the third day, and is alive today. Jesus, I receive you now as my Lord and Savior, Amen"!

If you have said this prayer, you are now a new creation in Christ Jesus! Now go and share the good news with someone! You have now been adopted into a new family! Here are a few things you can do as a new member of Jesus' family. Get a bible of your own and read it daily to get understanding of the word of God; to renew your mind; to get encouragement, and much more. (2 Timothy 3:16).

Pray. Prayer allows us to communicate with God and develop a personal relationship with Him. It's how we receive answers to our problems; how to overcome our spiritual battles; how not to be anxious, and so much more. There are many reasons why we should develop a prayer life and these are just a few. (Mark 11:24).

You can also find a church to join. It is good to connect with other believers to encourage one another, to worship God, and to hear the teaching of the Gospel. Now that you are saved, share what God has done in your life with others so that they too, can believe and desire to come to know this awesome God that saved you. Others need salvation too. There are many hurting people in the world who need hope. (1 Timothy 4:13).

Be ever encouraged in your Lord and Savior, Jesus Christ. He loves you and has a great plan for your life (Jeremiah 29:11).

CHAPTER 8

Finding Closure

EVEN THOUGH MANY years have now passed by, my biological father and I had never had a heart to heart talk about our relationship as father and daughter, until now.

Recently, the Lord laid it on my heart that it was time to address my past issues concerning my father. Even while I was writing this book, I knew the Lord was ready to bring closure and healing to this area of my life. I realized I was harboring bitter feelings and resentment toward my dad after all these years.

With the help of the Lord one day, I got up the nerve to talk with my dad. I admitted to my dad how I had truly felt over the years about his physical and emotional absence from my life. As I confessed of how not having him in my life in my younger years made me feel, streams of tears began to roll down my face. It was such a relief to finally tell him how I had felt all those years.

After telling him all that was in my heart, I heard Jesus telling me to hug him. My dad opened his arms wide, embraced me, and told me he loved me too. He said he always had. I needed to hear him say that because for years, I had felt like a fatherless child or like a child no father had wanted. That was a horrible feeling, one that no one should go through life enduring.

Not many days after talking with my dad, I began having a sense of peace in this area of my life. I have been his caregiver for about seven years now due to his stroke; he had been in my life, but it felt as if he had been miles away until we talked.

Today my father and I are taking things a day at a time. I am now healing from the wounds of the past of not having a close relationship with him over the years. It's a process, but it's one I'm grateful for. My dad has quite a sense of humor. I had never realized how funny he was. I guess I had always thought it was sarcasm. We still butt heads occasionally, but we often do it with humor. He has his own way of showing me he loves me. He is not a person of many words or affectionate, but I get it—he's not perfect, but he does the best he can. I know he cares, and that's enough for me.

Through a lesson of love and forgiveness from the Lord, I learned to forgive myself, my father, and others. The same way that the Spirit of the Lord helped me to release my heart's issues about my father, He also helped me forgive the individual who abused me. Not many years after I had left that abusive relationship, the person who abused me called me and asked me to forgive him. He was remorseful for what he had done to me and asked if I would be willing to forgive him. At the time I said yes. I had gone through years thinking I had actually forgiven him for what he had done to me, but from time to time, I could still feel anger and rage every time I heard of someone being abused by their partner or even killed. My mind would often go back to what my ex-boyfriend did to me. It would stir up anger within me. I didn't realize it at the time, but that was an indication that I hadn't quite healed or had truly forgiven him.

The Lord revealed to me that I hadn't quite forgiven him and that I was still holding onto what I had suffered years before. I realized that deep inside I was still having feelings of animosity towards my ex-boyfriend. We can sometimes think we have forgiven a person but we can actually still be having feelings of bitterness and resentment toward an individual without realizing it. If I wanted to help others in abusive situations, I had to decide to let go of my past hurts and forgive him. When I made a decision to release the animosity in my heart, that time around, I meant it, and the Lord began to heal the wounds in my heart that I had been carrying for many years. In turn, I was able to pray for this individual and mean it.

Without the Lord's help, I wouldn't have been able to forgive him. I encourage those who have or are suffering from abuse to seek counseling and be truthful about how you feel after leaving the abusive relationship because if you're not careful, you could began to see all men or women as the enemy. The scripture of Ephesians 6:12 helped me to understand the real enemy behind abuse. The word of God has really helped me understand the struggles that I have faced in my life. The more that I renew my mind through the word of God, the more I know that I have the victory in Christ Jesus as do all of God's people!

CHAPTER 9

My Third Father

I CAN REMEMBER a time when it seemed that nothing in my life made any sense. Everything felt so out of order and I was broken from many issues in my life, to the point of contemplating on taking my life.

It wasn't until I was healed, delivered and transformed in the presence of this amazing God who I now call Father God. I call Him Father God because that's who He became to me when I needed the love of a Father the most. I thank God for having two earthly fathers who love me, but it would take the love of my Third and Heavenly Father to reveal to me what love, forgiveness, and healing was really all about.

I asked myself the question of *"why did it take me getting to know this awesome God before things would finally make sense in my life"*? I found my answer in the Lord. I discovered that in His presence, I could not remain in the same state of brokenness as I had always been in. It is something about being in the presence of the Lord that will not allow you to stay the same mentally, emotionally, nor spiritually. I received total healing from the wounds of my past; total freedom from harboring anger and resentment towards others; and total deliverance from emotional baggage, and self-esteem issues.

As I wrote this chapter of the book, the number three came to mind. As I thought about the number three, I thought about what it represents. In many ways, the number three represents a form of completeness. Here are a few examples of the significance of the number three in the Bible: It was the third hour when Jesus was crucified (Mark 15:25). Jesus was resurrected on the third day (Luke 24:1-8). Three people witnessed Jesus's transfiguration on Mount Hermon – James, John, and Peter (Matthew 17:1-2). God is in the form of three persons – Father, Son, and the Holy Spirit (Matthew 28:19).

In Jesus, I feel that I am complete. Through my encounter with the Lord came healing, deliverance, and understanding. As He began to heal the broken places in my life, I found that I was able to really love the Lord, myself, and others. The more He healed me of my internal scars and emotional baggage, the more I was able to forgive.

I believe that before the beginning of time, it was ordained that I would come to know God through His Son, Jesus. It was no surprise to God that these particular situations and circumstances with my earthly fathers had had such an impact on my life the way that they did. It was also no surprise to God that these same set of circumstances played a role in my drawing closer to Him.

During that time, I felt like the Lord was taking me on a journey of truly getting to know Him. When I called Him my Savior, Redeemer, Provider, Protector, and Healer, I began to realize that this was not just casual talk or some song that I was singing to the Lord, but that each name I called him had actual meaning behind the word.

I know Jesus as my Savior because He has saved me in many ways, but most important, He saved me from being lost and living a life without Him. After living with blinders on, I began to see things clearly through His righteousness and His Word. I know Him as my Redeemer because I was redeemed—bought by the great price He had paid on the cross for our redemption. I know Him as my Protector because He protected me from losing my life in a violent domestic relationship, and He protected me and my kids when we felt unsafe. Jesus is my Provider because when I lost my job and was out of work for several years, He made a way for me and my family to continue to have a home, food, and clothing.

I never had to ask anyone for anything because the Lord would make sure that my kids and I had plenty of what we needed. He would often use different people at times to become blessings to me and my family, and He repeatedly opened doors to resources; this is why I am confident in saying He is my Provider. He made possible in the open what I prayed to Him for in secret. I know Jesus is my Healer because He healed my body of arthritis through my prayers and having faith in Him. I trusted Him through His Word to take care of me. Knowing God is with you when you face life's battles will take your faith in Him to a much higher level.

As the Lord revealed and healed my brokenness, He helped me realize that neither of my earthly fathers were perfect but that they had done the best they could for my sisters and I at the time. They cared for us, provided for us, and loved us in their own way and as best they knew how. I knew that they were not perfect but it was unfair of me to try to hold them at a standard where I felt that they should have been.

I also realized that my biological father had broken places in his own life and that it was important that I forgive him for not being there for me in the ways I felt he should have been. My dad had suffered some traumatic things when he was a child too; he didn't receive all of the love and attention that he needed in his youth, thus creating issues later on in his life.

My father did the best he could for us girls, but at the same time, I believe we all have room to grow. We can all do better as parents, spouses, friends, and even children. We often want others to change their bad habits and mature in many ways while we ourselves may not want to change or think we're never the problem. We all have flaws, but we can all change for the better.

It's hard to love someone when you don't love yourself, or have ever really been shown or given much love, but we all can get help in those areas where we are broken so that in turn we can become better people and learn how to love and care for others better. We as human beings can strive to love as our heavenly Father does. It is good for us to learn to forgive each other when we don't always get it right because each of us will eventually miss the mark at some point. That is one of the reasons we shouldn't hold others responsible for validating us and being there for us in every way we want them to be. We are imperfect people in an imperfect world. We all have been tainted in some way or another, and will at some point let others down.

Your parents are able to love you only so much. Your spouse is able to love and be there for you only so much. It's the same with your children, friends, and pastor. We should never put the responsibility on another to meet all our needs, or move heaven and earth for us. Human efforts can go only so far before we see a crack in the foundation, but with God, the foundation is stable (Psalm 46:1, 1 Corinthians 3:11).

In no way am I saying human beings aren't capable of loving one another and being there to help care for one another because we can and we do a great job at it but it's a good thing to keep in mind that we shouldn't always expect others to measure up to our standards. Such high demands should not be placed on us. As human beings, we can strive to be there for one another and do the best we can, but we all need mercy, grace, and forgiveness from time to time. This is a lesson that I have had to learn to grasp over the last few years.

Many years ago before I developed a close relationship with the Lord, I used to look to people to save me from financial hardship, protect me from danger, and comfort me when I was depressed, stressed, or lonely. But today, it's a different story. No longer do I put that demand on others. I have a more healthy view of how to treat others and how to love them. I am grateful for my relationships with my parents, friends, and loved ones. I understand more now that if we can't always meet each other's need, then it is ok. We should still love one another regardless because that's what love is. My loved ones can be of great help but I put my total trust in the Lord for my weightiest problems.

The Lord is a comforter and can mend any broken heart. He give us peace that surpasses all understanding (Philippians 4:7). God's love endures forever. The Lord is the reason why I am grateful for many things in my life today but more importantly, I am grateful for my relationship with Him as my heavenly Father. This is the God I have come to know and love, and I enjoy sharing Him with anyone who will listen.

CHAPTER 10

Being Made Whole and Complete

A S CHILDREN OF God, we are all constantly being shaped and molded into the image of Christ Jesus; we are works in progress. Out of my heart came the issues of my life, but I am thankful the Lord is constantly bringing deliverance, healing, wholeness, and completeness to every area of my life. When we are born into this world, we don't get to choose our parents or family. We don't get to choose whether we come into a home of wealth or poverty. We don't get to choose the situations or circumstances we are dealt in this life. No matter how tough life gets, one thing I know for sure is that God causes all things to work together for the good for those who love Him (Romans 8:28).

The scripture of Proverbs 4:23 tells me to guard my heart with all diligence-so I now try to be careful of what enters my heart as well as keep a check of what comes out of it. The heart is naturally deceitful, but we can guard it through prayer, repentance, forgiveness and studying the Word of God. I can't stop the actions of others, change the past, or avoid what life brings my way, but I can make the conscious decision to forgive, release past hurts, pray, and cast my cares and burdens on the Lord.

I understand now more than ever that none of us are perfect. Guarding our hearts from resentment and bitterness is critical. For years, my heart was unguarded, and it was open and vulnerable to betrayal, rejection, lies, deception, abandonment, unforgiveness, and bitterness, which created many of the issues that I had to face in my life. Not guarding our hearts can provoke us to retaliate, pay back evil for evil, harbor evil thoughts, and so on. We can't prevent certain things from happening to us, but we can choose to forgive and love in spite of them. It's easier said than done most times, but it can be done. We can choose to rise above life's devastating situations and circumstances and take back our joy and peace.

I couldn't have chosen a father who would have given me all the love I needed while growing up; that was beyond my control. I didn't choose this situation; it chose me. I had no choice but to endure the situation that caused my father not to be in my life. I understand now that whatever hardships come my way, I must decide to not allow myself to become bitter or harbor resentment toward anyone. Harboring unforgiveness can cause physical sickness as well as spiritual sickness.

For many years, I carried the hurt in my heart caused by what had happened, and that resulted in high blood pressure and depression. At the time, I didn't realize how important it was to turn my issues over to the Lord, who knew exactly what to do with them. No matter what happens to us in this life; the issues that result from the experience are not meant to define us. We are meant to overcome every painful experience that life brings our way. The word of God says that we are more than conquerors through Christ, who loves us (Romans 8:37).

All my ups, downs, rejections, and issues of life played a part in who I am today. We grow through the pains of life. We become stronger when we overcome our issues. No one but God kept me from losing my mind during the hardest times in my life. Praise be to my Lord and Savior, Jesus Christ.

God never promised we wouldn't have trials or issues, but He promised to never leave us nor forsake us (Deuteronomy 31:6). He has faithfully seen me through every problem and He will do the same for you. God causes all things to work together for the good, and that means all things including every letdown, abandonment, loss, false accusation, mistreatment, disappointment, betrayal, and every other bad thing we suffer.

God can use every bit of our hurt and pain to give us beauty for ashes (Isaiah 61:3). God does not waste any experience. We are taught lessons through all our life experiences. We may not always understand why such hurtful things happen to us or our loved ones, but I know they are not meant to destroy us. We have a testimony of what we have been through in our lives and in turn, I believe it is meant to be shared with others to give hope that they too can overcome.

In 2013, the Lord laid it upon my heart to start a women's ministry that would allow me to encourage women who have gone through similar struggles that I have. Today, I am a speaker on domestic violence. I bring awareness of this issue through my ministry. Helping women and men has given me such a sense of purpose. For once in my life, I feel I know what I was born to do. There's nothing like showing the love of Christ to others and helping them in whatever way Jesus leads me to do that. I enjoy seeing people's lives turn around for the better and witnessing their being set free from bondage.

I always tell the women at my speaking events that one of the best ways they can get the last laugh in the face of the enemy is to allow God to take what the devil meant for evil and turn it into good. The enemy thinks that he has us down for the count when our lives are disrupted by unfortunate events, but once we rise up out of the ashes of life, now we show our enemy that we have the victory over our circumstances! As overcomers, we must help others overcome by sharing our testimony of how God brought us through (Revelation 12:11). I believe that the more we share our testimonies, the more we are set free.

Today, I am free from low self-esteem issues, abandonment issues, domestic violence issues, and emotional baggage. Jesus set me free in every way a person can be set free. Even today, He is still setting me free in areas of my life that I didn't know I needed to be set free from. Who the Lord sets free is free indeed (John 8:36). With the help of the Lord, I have taken back every bit of my joy, peace, and happiness that the enemy had stolen from me over the years. It feels so good to know that we as Christians, are not defeated but that we have been given the authority through Christ Jesus to trample upon serpents and scorpions and over all power of the enemy (Luke 10:19)! I thank God for my renewed mind and outlook on life. God never ceases to amaze me. We are all works in progress, but I am convinced He simply wants each of us to live our best life on this earth without all the emotional, physical, and mental issues weighing us down. He also intends for us to be a blessing to one another, encourage one another, pray for one another, and most important of all, love one another.

No matter what situations and circumstances you are dealing with, please know that there is hope. I found my hope in the Lord. Life is not always easy, but God is good. I found out over the years that there is no problem too big that God cannot handle, nor is there a problem too small that does not concern Him. If it concerns you, it concerns God. He cares deeply about us and the problems we face. His love is everlasting and His grace is sufficient for us. Today, I am in a much happier and peaceful place more so than I've ever been before, and I give all thanks and praise to my Lord and Savior, Jesus Christ.

We cannot help what life brings our way or how people treat us, but we can choose to forgive and release the hurt and pains of life so we won't go around carrying burdens and dealing with the consequences or aftermath of what's in our hearts years later. We must not allow people or circumstances to rob us of our joy or to keep us from living the lives God intended us to have. I pray that you will be encouraged in whatever circumstances that you may be facing today. You are not alone. There is hope in the Lord. He will faithfully see you through life's trials if you will put your trust in Him. Above all else, guard your heart with all diligence because out of the heart flows the issues of life (Proverbs 4:23).

ABOUT THE AUTHOR

HENRIETTA FREEMAN, A native of Greenville, South Carolina, grew up in downtown Greenville with five siblings. She attended and graduated from Berea High School. She earned an A.A.S degree in medical administration at ECPI College of Technology. She is now a minister called to do the work of the Lord, and she is the founder of Healing Waters (Center for Abused Women). Henrietta is a survivor of domestic violence and is a speaker on domestic violence. She is a mother of two wonderful kids, a facilitator, and an entrepreneur.

She is passionate about helping encourage others through her ministry, writing and speaking. She hopes that through sharing her life trials, will give others hope and encouragement that they too can be healed from their past wounds and move forward to a great future that awaits them. She gives all credit to her Lord and Savior, Jesus Christ, who helped her overcome the hardest of her battles. She also credits the Lord for teaching her how to forgive on a much deeper level.

Today, she is mentally and emotionally stronger, wiser, more patient, less anxious, and more forgiving. She says, "The best way to get the last laugh in the face of the enemy is to allow God to take what the enemy meant for evil in your life and turn it around and use it for the good" and "What you survive should give hope to others."

Made in the USA
Columbia, SC
18 November 2021

49269906R00037